# CURIOSITY ROVER

## SEARCHING FOR LIFE ON MARS

### By John Hamilton

XTREME SPACECRAFT

A&D Xtreme
An imprint of Abdo Publishing | abdopublishing.com

abdopublishing.com

Published by Abdo Publishing, a division of ABDO, PO Box 398166, Minneapolis, Minnesota 55439. Copyright ©2018 by Abdo Consulting Group, Inc. International copyrights reserved in all countries. No part of this book may be reproduced in any form without written permission from the publisher. A&D Xtreme™ is a trademark and logo of Abdo Publishing.

Printed in the United States of America, North Mankato, MN.
032017
052017

Editor: Sue Hamilton
Graphic Design: Sue Hamilton
Cover Design: Candice Keimig
Cover Photo: iStock
Interior Photos: All photos NASA.

Websites
To learn more about Xtreme Spacecraft, visit abdobooklinks.com. These links are routinely monitored and updated to provide the most current information available.

Publisher's Cataloging-in-Publication Data

Names: Hamilton, John, author.
Title: Curiosity Rover: searching for life on Mars / by John Hamilton.
Other titles: Searching for life on Mars
Description: Minneapolis, MN : Abdo Publishing, 2018. | Series: Xtreme spacecraft | Includes index.
Identifiers: LCCN 2016962223 | ISBN 9781532110092 (lib. bdg.) | ISBN 9781680787948 (ebook)
Subjects: LCSH: Mars (Planet)--Exploration--Juvenile literature. | Life on other planets--Exploration--Juvenile literature.
Classification: DDC 523--dc23
LC record available at http://lccn.loc.gov/2016962223

# CONTENTS

# SEARCHING FOR LIFE ON MARS

**Mars is a bone-chillingly cold and dry planet. It seems impossible that any creature could live there. But in its distant past, water flowed across its surface.**

 *XTREME FACT – Wild temperature swings regularly occur on Mars. Typical daytime highs might reach 70 degrees Fahrenheit (21° C), but then at night plunge to minus 100 degrees Fahrenheit (-73° C). The average Martian temperature is minus 80 degrees Fahrenheit (-62° C).*

About 3.5 billion years ago, the air was thicker and warmer, perhaps Earth-like. How can we know if life sprang up there? Could humans live on Mars today? To answer these questions, NASA's Curiosity rover arrived in 2012 to hunt for clues in the Martian rocks.

A self-portrait taken by the Curiosity rover on Mars at the Mojave site.

# MARS ROVER HISTORY

The first rover on Mars was NASA's Sojourner. It landed in 1997. It was about the size of a large microwave oven. Its mission was to take photos of the Martian surface and study soil and rocks. To cushion its landing, Sojourner used a parachute plus a protective cocoon of airbags.

Sojourner studies the rock named Yogi shortly after landing on Mars, the Red Planet, in 1997. It explored the planet for about 3 months.

Spirit took the first color photos of another planet by a rover. Spirit continued to send information to Earth for years. After getting stuck in soft soil in late 2009, it finally stopped communicating with NASA on March 22, 2010.

The next two Mars rovers were named Spirit and Opportunity. These golf-cart-sized mobile laboratories landed in 2004. Both rovers lasted for many years beyond their expected life spans.

As of January 2017, Opportunity has driven more than 27 miles (43.5 km) on the surface of Mars. This is far more than any other rover. It continues to send data to NASA.

# PLANNING AND BUILDING

In the early 2000s, NASA engineers began planning a new Mars rover. It would carry more science instruments and be much larger than previous rovers. It was named Curiosity. It was designed to study the Martian climate and geology.

Scientists stand next to three duplicate Mars rovers at NASA's Jet Propulsion Lab in California.

Spirit/Opportunity

Sojourner

NASA wanted to find out if Mars ever supported life. The space agency also wanted to prove it could safely land large rovers. The lessons learned would help future Mars missions.

Curiosity

*XTREME FACT – Clara Ma, a sixth-grader from Kansas, won an essay contest to name the new Curiosity rover. She wrote, "Curiosity is the passion that drives us through our everyday lives."*

# THE MSL SPACECRAFT

The Curiosity rover was carried to the Red Planet aboard the Mars Science Laboratory (MSL) spacecraft. The spacecraft also included computers, fuel, rockets, a heat shield for entering Mars's atmosphere, and a large parachute.

The MSL spacecraft's large heat shield has a diameter of 14.8 feet (4.5 m).

**XTREME FACT** – *After pieces of the MSL were tested, they were shipped to a clean room at the Jet Propulsion Laboratory and installed in the spacecraft and rover.*

It was assembled at NASA's Jet Propulsion Laboratory (JPL) in Pasadena, California. It took several years to build and test all the parts and computer software needed for a successful flight to distant Mars.

The MSL Spacecraft at NASA's Jet Propulsion Laboratory.

# THE ROVER

The Curiosity rover is about the size of a small car. It has six wide wheels that help it move over obstacles.

Mobility testing is conducted on Curiosity in 2011. The rover is 10 feet (3 m) long, 9 feet (2.7 m) wide, and 7 feet (2.1 m) high. It weighs 1,982 pounds (899 kg).

The rover gets its power from a radioisotope power system. Heat generated by radioactive plutonium-238 is converted to electricity. Two identical computers control the rover. If one computer shuts down, the backup takes over. Curiosity can send radio signals directly to Earth. It also communicates with satellites that orbit Mars, which then relay messages to Earth.

Curiosity has 17 cameras. Some are for taking high-resolution photos of the Martian landscape, or for driving around hazards. The other cameras have special purposes. Some analyze rock samples. Rocks can also be analyzed using lasers and x-rays.

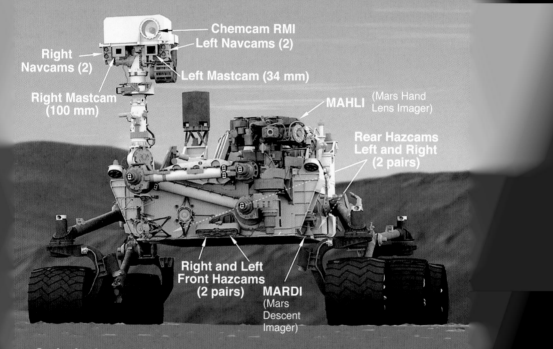

Chemcam RMI
Left Navcams (2)

Right
Navcams (2)

Left Mastcam (34 mm)

Right Mastcam
(100 mm)

MAHLI (Mars Hand
Lens Imager)

Rear Hazcams
Left and Right
(2 pairs)

Right and Left
Front Hazcams
(2 pairs)

MARDI
(Mars
Descent
Imager)

Curiosity has navigation, scientific analysis, and photo cameras.

*XTREME FACT – There is a radiation detector aboard Curiosity. Scientists discovered that even a short manned mission would be hazardous to humans. Future astronauts will need shielding to protect them.*

Curiosity has a camera, drill, and scoop on its robotic arm. It can study rocks, drill into them, and scoop up powdered samples. The samples are moved to chemistry labs inside the rover.

Curiosity's robotic arm works at Mount Remarkable in April 2014.

# LAUNCH

The Mars Science Laboratory spacecraft, with the Curiosity rover aboard, was launched on November 26, 2011. An Atlas V rocket was used to send the MSL into space. The launch site was Cape Canaveral Air Force Station in Florida. The trip to Mars took more than eight months and covered about 352 million miles (566 million km).

**XTREME FACT** – The Atlas V rocket used for the MSL spacecraft was a two-stage launch vehicle. With the MSL aboard, the Atlas V's height was 191 feet (58 m), and it weighed about 1.17 million pounds (530,703 kg).

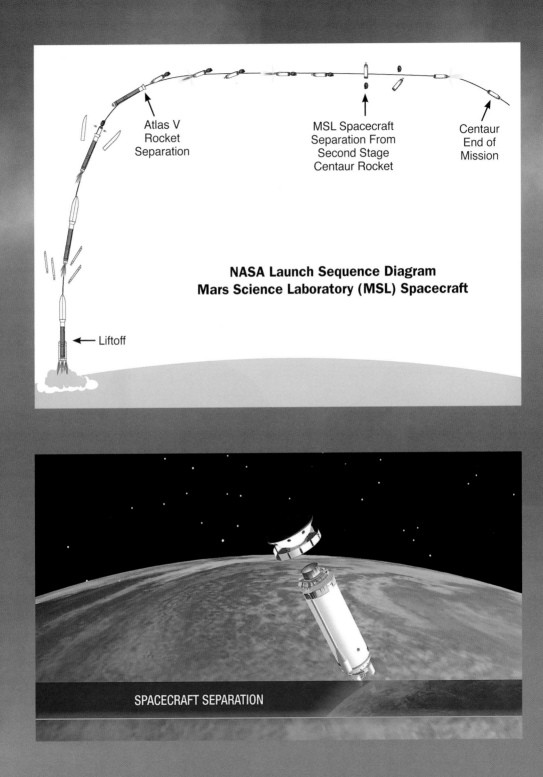

NASA Launch Sequence Diagram
Mars Science Laboratory (MSL) Spacecraft

Atlas V
Rocket
Separation

MSL Spacecraft
Separation From
Second Stage
Centaur Rocket

Centaur
End of
Mission

Liftoff

SPACECRAFT SEPARATION

# LANDING ON MARS

Curiosity landed on Mars automatically. On August 5, 2012, the Mars Science Laboratory spacecraft dropped into the planet's atmosphere. It fired small rockets to guide it to the landing zone. Its speed reached more than 13,000 miles per hour (20,921 km/hr).

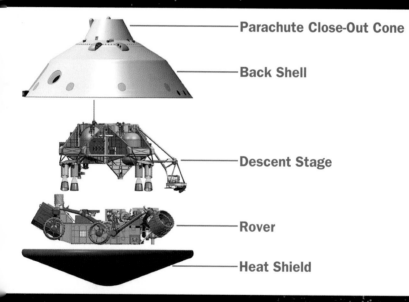

- Parachute Close-Out Cone
- Back Shell
- Descent Stage
- Rover
- Heat Shield

*XTREME FACT – The Mars Science Laboratory's heat shield reached extreme temperatures up to 3,800 degrees Fahrenheit (2,093 degrees Celsius). Inside, Curiosity stayed cool at about 50 degrees Fahrenheit (10 degrees Celsius).*

The friction of speeding through the Martian atmosphere created intense heat. The metal heat shield on the bottom of the spacecraft protected the rover.

About 7 miles (11 km) above the ground, the spacecraft's speed dropped to 900 miles per hour (1,448 kph). A large parachute billowed out, and the heat shield popped off.

Then the top shell and the parachute were ejected. Eight rockets fired. The spacecraft slowed even more. In the final seconds, the Curiosity rover was lowered to the ground by three 21-foot (6.4-m) -long nylon ropes.

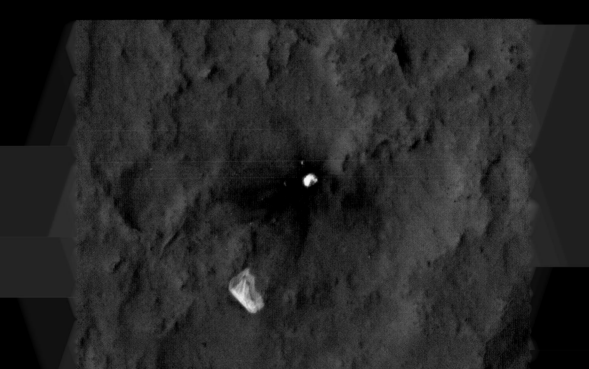

A photo of the parachute and back shell that helped deliver the Curiosity rover to Mars. The image was taken on August 6, 2012, by NASA's Mars Reconnaissance Orbiter circling the Red Planet.

 *XTREME FACT – Unlike previous rovers, Curiosity was too big and heavy to safely use airbags. The airbags would have popped or been shredded by rocks, causing damage to the rover.*

Curiosity's "sky crane" maneuver was very complicated. Many things could have gone wrong. But it was necessary to keep the rover far away from the spacecraft's rockets. Otherwise, the rockets would have stirred up dust and rocks on the Martian surface. The debris could have harmed the rover's electronic parts. After Curiosity reached the ground, it signaled its controllers on Earth. It was ready to start its mission.

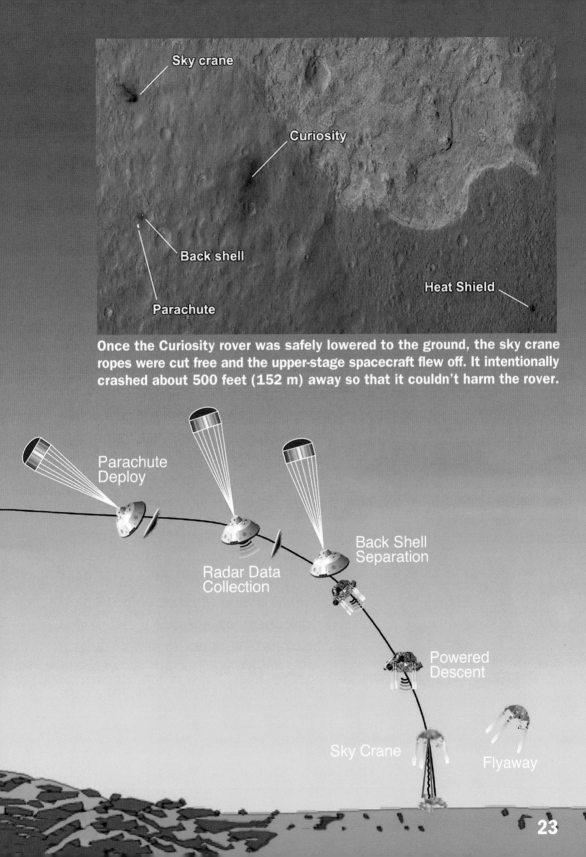

Sky crane

Curiosity

Back shell

Parachute

Heat Shield

Once the Curiosity rover was safely lowered to the ground, the sky crane ropes were cut free and the upper-stage spacecraft flew off. It intentionally crashed about 500 feet (152 m) away so that it couldn't harm the rover.

Parachute Deploy

Radar Data Collection

Back Shell Separation

Powered Descent

Sky Crane

Flyaway

# THE LANDING SITE

Curiosity landed in Gale Crater. It was formed billions of years ago when a large meteor slammed into Mars. Gale Crater is about the size of Rhode Island and Connecticut combined. It is 96 miles (154 km) in diameter.

Gale Crater & Landing Site

A large mountain, called Aeolis Mons (also known as Mount Sharp), rises about 18,000 feet (5,486 m) in the middle of the crater. NASA chose Gale Crater as Curiosity's landing site because there is evidence of ancient waterways flowing there.

← Mount Sharp

# STUDYING MARS

Curiosity soon began exploring Gale Crater, with instructions sent by Earth controllers. It analyzed nearby rocks. It collected soil and bedrock samples with its drill and scoop. In an ancient dry streambed it found evidence that long ago, liquid water—a necessary ingredient for life—flowed on the surface of Mars.

Curiosity made a drill hole to collect rock powder samples for testing.

Curiosity also found the key chemical building blocks of life in the Martian rocks. The elements included oxygen, hydrogen, carbon, sulfur, and phosphorus. Curiosity proved that microscopic life could have lived on Mars.

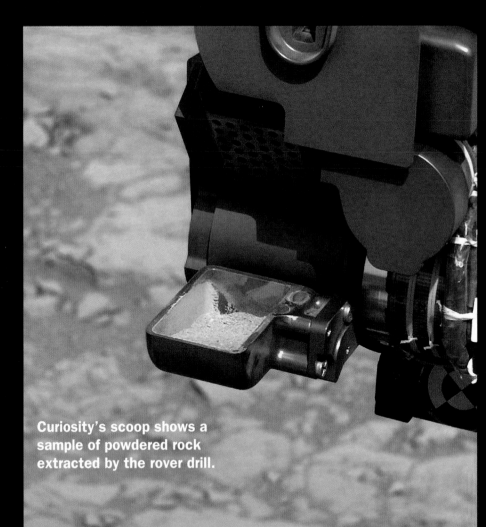

Curiosity's scoop shows a sample of powdered rock extracted by the rover drill.

# THE MISSION CONTINUES

In July 2013, Curiosity began a long journey to the base of Mount Sharp. Along the way, it studied more rocks. It also took many photos of the Red Planet. It arrived at Mount Sharp in September 2014, where it continues investigating the wet past of the Martian landscape.

Curiosity's wheels show the wear-and-tear of about 10 miles (16 km) of driving on Mars. The rover can travel up to 295 feet (90 m) per hour. Usually, however, it averages closer to 98 feet (30 m) per hour.

The Curiosity rover was supposed to last two years, but it has continued functioning far longer. As of 2017, it has been exploring Mars for more than twice its expected life span.

Curiosity scoops sand from Namib Dune for testing.

*XTREME FACT – The Curiosity robotic rover project employed hundreds of scientists from around the world, and cost about $2.5 billion. That is more money than previous rover missions, but far less than the planned future missions to send humans to Mars.*

# GLOSSARY

**AIRBAG**

A cloth bag in a vehicle that rapidly inflates during a crash to protect passengers or equipment.

**BEDROCK**

Hard, solid rock usually covered by loose soil or sand.

**CLEAN ROOM**

A special room where delicate electronic equipment is assembled in a dust-free environment.

**NATIONAL AERONAUTICS AND SPACE ADMINISTRATION (NASA)**

A United States government space agency started in 1958. NASA's goals include space exploration, as well as increasing people's understanding of Earth, our solar system, and the universe.

## ORBIT

The circular path a moon or spacecraft makes when traveling around a planet or other large celestial body. There are several satellites that orbit Mars, including NASA's Mars Reconnaissance Orbiter and the European Space Agency's ExoMars Trace Gas Orbiter.

## PLUTONIUM-238

A highly radioactive element that produces heat. The heat is converted to electricity in a radioisotope power system, such as the one used on the Curiosity rover. This system is more reliable than the solar panels used on previous Mars rovers, such as Sojourner. When solar panels become covered in Martian dust, it lowers the amount of power produced. Radioisotope power systems produce steady, uninterrupted amounts of electricity, often for decades.

## ROVER

A robotic vehicle that is driven over rough terrain by remote control.